NO OTHER WAY
BUT TO
TRUST AND OBEY!

LON ECKDAHL

Printed in the United States of America

First Printing Edition, 2024 I

I S B N 979-8-3305-6236-7

Acknowledgments

I would like to acknowledge and thank two very special ladies. First of all, my wife, who has been extremely supportive of the book. I would also like to thank Sharon Schuur, who did the proofreading and made several suggestions that made the manuscript much better.

About The Author

Lon Eckdahl has been a pastor for more than 55 years. He has also served as a teacher, law enforcement chaplain, including service with the FBI, and a camp speaker, and chairman for a Billy Graham Crusade with associate evangelist John Wesley White. Lon and his wife, Diana, have four grown children 12 grandchildren, and two great-grandchildren. They make their home in the Northwest. Lon loved being a pastor. Three directives brought focus to his ministry: Love God – Love the people – and preach the Word! He is extremely grateful for the privilege of proclaiming the simplicity of the gospel and the wonderful love God has showered on us all.

Contents

Acknowledgments ii

About The Author iii

Contents iv

Chapter 1: The Simplicity Of The Gospel..1

Chapter 2: No Other Way 9

Chapter 3: What Does It Mean To Trust? 13

Chapter 4: To Obey Or Not To Obey, That Is The Question? 21

Chapter 5: God Is Pro-Choice.. 31

Chapter 6: Postscript.. 35

Chapter 1:
The Simplicity Of The Gospel

I was impacted by the simplicity of the gospel in my very first pastorate when I met a young Korean man named Chang Ho Lee. A friend of mine had called and encouraged me to have this young man come to our church and give his testimony. I didn't know anything about him, but I went ahead and agreed.

Chang Ho Lee was a teenager in Korea during the Korean War. During the war, his parents had been killed, and so he found himself as an orphan on the streets. He joined together with other boys who had also lost their parents. This group of boys stayed close to a United States military base that was nearby so they could find food in the garbage cans that were a part of the base. A great deal of food was thrown away daily.

Chang Ho Lee had no religious background at all. In fact, during this time he came to the conclusion that Jesus Christ was one of the worst human beings who had ever lived because his name was used as a swearword among the American soldiers. On a side note, no other religious leader in our history has ever had his name used as a swear word.

During his time on the streets, Chang Ho Lee committed numerous crimes, mostly theft. But one day he was caught, and placed in jail. While in jail he was confined to his cell. The only opportunity to leave his cell was to choose to attend a Christian worship service on Sunday mornings which was conducted by a military chaplain. So, Chang Ho Lee, desperate to get a reprieve from his cell started attending. This was the first time he heard the truth about who Jesus Christ really was.

One Sunday morning, the chaplain had some small New Testament bibles, supplied by The Gideon, that he was handing out for free. Chang Ho Lee took one, and when he got back to his cell he discovered that the thin paper this little Bible was printed on was perfect for rolling his cigarettes. So one by one he began tearing out the pages, rolling his tobacco, and smoking them. As time went by, Chang Ho Lee had smoked through Matthew, Mark, and Luke, and he had recently started John.

One night, in the dark, as he was getting ready to smoke a page, a guard hit him with a flashlight and said, "What are you doing?" Chang Ho Lee responded, "I'm reading my New Testament." The guard asked, "What are you reading?" And Lee began to read at the top of the page these words, "God so loved the world that He gave His One and

Only Son that whoever believes in Him should not perish, but have everlasting life." The guard shrugged his shoulders and went on his way. Lee proceeded to smoke the page, but the words he had read began to haunt him. Was there really a God who loved him? Was God really offering him eternal life if he would believe? And so, on that next Sunday morning in the worship service Chang Ho Lee committed his life to Jesus Christ! He was forever changed, and as he began to study the Bible, he actually felt that God was calling him to be a missionary to the United States. And that's how I met him.

Oh, the simplicity of the gospel! I have always been in awe of the simplicity of the great plan God has for His creation. We have a God who is unique in so many ways. There are many facets to His personality. He is loving and compassionate. But He is also just. He deeply loves His creation, but He hates the ugliness of sin. His divine plan for His creation is all about relationships. He created man in order to have a relationship with man. Then He gave the man a woman with whom the man was to share life with. And out of that relationship came children, and the family was born. All of that is so beautiful; so beautiful that it is actually hard to define it or to describe it. The psalmist declares in Psalm 50:2 "From Zion, perfect in beauty, God shines forth."

But with all of the beauty that surrounds our God, we must also recognize that He holds us accountable to the righteous standard that is a part of that beauty. When God created man, He created him in His own image. Man was not created to automatically carry out all that God envisioned for him, like a puppet on a string. God created man with the freedom to choose. A man had the God-given ability to choose what God desired for him, or he could choose to reject the wonderful plan God had for him.

It reminds me of what happens when we choose to partner with God in the procreation of our own children. When they are born, we have certain expectations for them. Do those expectations always come to fruition? Not likely! Our own children often make choices that do not bring us happiness. Often those choices bring us great sorrow. But nevertheless, these choices are theirs to make. And so it is in our relationship with our heavenly Father. Every day we have choices to make, and our lives are the product of those choices.

So in essence, as God watched man reject His commands, given in love, sin entered the picture. God not only had a problem with sin, He actually detested it because it was totally contrary to His righteousness. The Bible clearly teaches us that our God is a Holy God. And when we allow sin to become a part of our lives, that sin actually causes a separation from this Holy God. But God, in His great love, developed a plan by which mankind could re-enter this relationship that He yearned for us to enjoy.

So what was God's plan? First of all, mankind needed to understand what God's righteousness really looked like, so God outlined for us what His righteous standard really looked like. We call it The Ten Commandments. These commandments clearly outline for us the difference between good choices and bad choices. God also plainly laid out for us the penalties for breaking His righteous standard. In order to be recipients of God's forgiveness, there had to be a penalty. And that penalty demanded a blood sacrifice. Therefore, all through the Old Testament, we see the sacrifices of blood carried out by God's priests. Sheep, bulls, goats, and birds, all were used in the sacrificial system.

But all of that was just the beginning of God's wonderful plan of redemption. God made it clear in the Old Testament that the sacrificial system was just the beginning of the plan He had in mind. There was coming a day, in the future, when a Messiah, a Redeemer, would come, and God's plan for redemption would be fully completed. Hebrews 10:10 says, "And by that will, we have been made holy through the sacrifice of the body of Jesus Christ once and for all."

Well, a little over two thousand years ago, a baby was miraculously born to a virgin girl who would change everything. He was born in the most humble of circumstances, and grew up in the midst of the most common of people, in a town many people looked down on, named Nazareth. He lived a very ordinary life for the first thirty years of His life.

At the age of thirty, the day came when the last of the Old Testament prophets, John the Baptist, pointed to Jesus and declared, "Look, the Lamb of God who takes away the sin of the world." (John 1:29) And so Jesus began His ministry, an earthly ministry that lasted a mere three years. The ending of His earthly life was just as miraculous as the beginning. It seemed so tragic at the time, but according to prophecy, Jesus fulfilled all of the demands of the Law. He became the supreme sacrifice as He shed His divine blood on an old rugged cross.

So now the way has been opened for us to enter into a dynamic relationship with our God without shedding the blood of lambs, goats, or any other kind of animal. God's divine Son was willing to enter our world in love, to give His life as a ransom for us, on an old rugged cross. All we must do is embrace the gift He has made available to us and enjoy the love of a heavenly Father who is at work for our good and His glory in everything that life throws at us.

So, with all of that background, consider with me the simplicity of this glorious gospel. In our world today, there are so many religions to consider. But every one of them, outside of Christianity, makes religion something that we must work for and sacrifice for. They all depend on what we do, while Christianity depends on what God has already done! God offers to each and every one of us His free gift of grace, made available through His Son Jesus Christ. And it's not so much a religion as it is a relationship. And oh, what a glorious relationship it is!

The Bible makes it very clear just how simple God's plan is for our salvation. This is reflected in the words of Paul and Silas in Acts 16:31: "Believe in the Lord Jesus, and you will be saved." And Romans 10:9-10 says, "If you confess with your mouth, 'Jesus is Lord,' and believe in your heart that God raised Him from the dead, you will be saved. For it is with your heart that you believe and are justified, and it is with your mouth that you confess and are saved."

You see, salvation, the forgiveness of our sins, is based on four simple truths:

1. God loves us and desires a personal relationship with every one of us.

2. But the reality is, that sin has separated us from our heavenly Father, and therefore we are unable to experience a relationship with Him.

3. In an expression of His love, God sent Jesus to our world and He became the sacrifice that made atonement for our sin, and because of His death on the cross, the gift of His amazing grace has been offered to every one of us.

4. However, His gift of grace is not automatic, we must reach out in confession and repentance of our sin to receive it. A gift is never a gift until it is received! It is my choice to receive God's gift that makes it a reality!

QUESTIONS FOR DISCUSSION

1. Have you ever considered just how simple God's plan of salvation is?

2. And since this gospel is so personal, have you ever considered making Him your Lord and Savior?

3. Remember this: God has voted for me; Satan has voted against me; I must make the deciding vote!

Chapter 2:
No Other Way

The idea for this book came to me in one of the great hymns of the church, "Trust and Obey." The chorus of that hymn says: "Trust and Obey, for there's no other way, to be happy in Jesus, but to Trust and Obey." Trust and Obey; These two words are oh-so simple, but they are also oh-so true! My relationship with Jesus needs to be the central focus of my life! And in order for that to be true, I must completely trust in Him; and I must be totally committed in obedience to His will for my life.

Jesus made it very clear to His disciples that there was only one way to really know the Father, and that was by faith in the Son. There truly is NO OTHER WAY! He said to His disciples in John 14:6 "I am the Way and the Truth and the Life. No one comes to the Father except through me."

The Apostle Paul writes in Philippians 2:9-11 "Therefore God exalted Him to the highest place and gave Him the name that is above every name, that at the name of Jesus, every knee should bow, in heaven and on earth and under the earth, and every tongue confess that Jesus Christ is Lord, to the glory of God the Father." Have you as yet made the confession that Jesus Christ is Lord, if you haven't, you will. It's better now than later.

In the Book of Hebrews, it is made clear that the access we now have to God is through Jesus. Hebrews 4:14 "Therefore, since we have a great high priest who has gone through the heavens, Jesus the Son of God, let us hold firmly to the faith we profess."

The Apostle John writes in I John 4:15 "If anyone acknowledges that Jesus is the Son of God, God lives in him and he in God." When Jesus prayed His high priestly prayer for us just before going to the cross, which is recorded for us in the 17th chapter of John's gospel, He defines for us the essence of eternal life in verse three when He says, "Now this is eternal life: that they may know You, the only true God, and Jesus Christ, whom You have sent."

In II Corinthians 11:3 Paul warned the Corinthians about losing the simplicity that is in our relationship with Jesus. He writes, "But I fear, lest by any means, as the serpent beguiled Eve through his subtlety, so your minds should be corrupted from the simplicity that is in Christ." (KJV) Don't allow your relationship with Jesus to lose its simplicity. The world around us is getting increasingly complex and is drifting farther and farther away from God. Ask yourself, "Do

I sense that Christ is with me every day and in every situation?" There is a danger that we can be involved in things about Christ and fail to live in the context of our relationship with Him.

The Apostle Paul made it clear that he had only one message. He writes in I Corinthians 2:2 "For I resolved to know nothing while I was with you except Jesus Christ and Him crucified." He reiterated that in chapter three, verse 11: "For no one can lay any foundation other than the one already laid, which is Jesus Christ."

There are so many religions in our world today, and there are many people who say, "Well, all religions end up in the same place, in heaven." But the Bible tells us that is not so. All roads do not lead to the same destination. Jesus Christ is the only way! Even if someone chooses not to believe that it doesn't make it any less true.

The words of the hymn "Trust and Obey" that really challenged me were: "Trust and obey for there is no other way to be happy in Christ Jesus, but to trust and obey." Now most people in our world are seeking to be happy. Usually, they are looking in the wrong places. But this hymn says, "No other way to be happy in Christ Jesus...." The happiness that we are challenged to possess is found in Christ Jesus. And yet there are still professing Christians who aren't really happy. The reason is – their failure to truly learn how to Trust and Obey!

There are those people who profess to be followers of Jesus and yet have not found fulfillment in that relationship. They may read their Bibles and go to church on occasion but still have not found true happiness in Christ. And that is just why those two little words, Trust and Obey, are so essential in our attempt to be true followers of Christ Jesus.

QUESTIONS FOR DISCUSSION

1. Have you considered the uniqueness that Jesus Christ is the only way to know God and to find your way to heaven?

2. Have you thought through the idea that those two words "Trust and Obey" encompass everything that is involved in truly following Jesus? There is nothing more!

Chapter 3:
What Does It Mean To Trust?

The dictionary defines trust as a "firm belief in the ability, or strength, of someone or something." So what does it mean to have "a firm belief?" To really believe that something is true means that any actions I may take relative to that something, will always reflect what I say I believe. The choices I make in living my life will always reflect what I believe to be true. A hypocrite is one whose actions do not back up what they say is true.

There is a story about a tightrope walker who was planning to cross Niagra Falls on a high wire. Before he did so he took a wheelbarrow and asked the crowd who had gathered, "How many believe that I can push this wheelbarrow across the Falls with a person in it?" Several people raised their hands. The tightrope walker turned to one of them and said, "Then get in the wheelbarrow!"

Trust not acted upon is not true trust!

I had a professor in college who used to say, "Faith is not something you have, it is something you do." There are a lot of things we may believe, but to really trust means that you are willing to exercise that belief; to put into action what you say you believe. I may believe that Jesus is a real person who actually lived on this earth, but to really trust in Him means to become a disciple of His, a follower of His precepts.

A group of Christians gathered to pray for rain, but only one brought an umbrella. His faith was expressed by what he did. When you throw babies in the air, they laugh because they know you will catch them. That is trust. Every night we go to bed without any assurance of being alive the next morning, but we still set the alarm to wake up – that is trust in the providence of God.

Consider the legal definition of the word "trust." A person, who may be called a "trustee," is given possession of property that belongs to someone else. The trustee makes decisions about this property in a way that will benefit the real owner. Something valuable is held in trust for the benefit of the real owner. Thinking about that in the spiritual sense, as Christians, we have been entrusted with something very valuable by God Himself – it is called the Gospel!

The gospel message had a high priority in the life of the Apostles. The Apostle Paul writes in I Thessalonians 2:4 "We speak as men approved by God to be entrusted with the gospel. We are not trying to please men but God, who tests our hearts." That word TRUST is a big word! In order to enter into this special relationship God has provided for me through what Jesus did on the cross I must trust in what He did for me.

When I think about what it means to trust, a mental picture comes to mind. I picture a father in a swimming pool encouraging his young son, who is standing on the edge of the pool, to jump into his arms. The child is afraid of the water, and doesn't know how to swim, but is challenged by the father to trust that he will catch him when he jumps. The trust that he has in his father supersedes his fear of the water.

There is a story about the simplicity of the trust our heavenly Father asks us to place in Him. It is the story of an electrical engineer who had never placed his trust in God, but who did accompany his family to church every Sunday. After listening to the pastor preach on the subject of trust, this man, as he left church one Sunday morning, asked the pastor if he could meet with him that next week. An appointment was made, and on the appointed day the man showed up at the pastor's office. The man said to the pastor, "I have been listening intently to your explanation of the gospel message and my problem is, it's just too simple! I am an electric engineer and the things of life are just not that simple. Life is very complicated. If the gospel message was a little more complicated, it would be easier for me to buy into it."

Since it was late in the afternoon and the pastor's office was becoming dark, the pastor asked the man, "Since you are an electric engineer, tell me what I need to do to get more light in here." The man responded, "Well that's easy enough, all you have to do is flip the light switch." The pastor said, "You are an electric engineer and you tell me that all I need to do is flip the switch. You of all people ought to know that in order for me to do that dams have to be built, and dynamos created, and wires strung from that dam to this city and to this church building before I can ever flip the switch." The electric engineer responded, "But all of that has been done." The pastor said, "So it is with the gospel – it's all been done. In Christ a dam has been built against God's judgment, a dynamo has been created in the power of the Holy Spirit, and Jesus, by His cross, has bridged the gap between that event and my life, and all I have to do is flip the switch and place my trust in what He has done for me on Calvary's cross." And that very afternoon, an electric engineer placed his faith in the Lord Jesus Christ! Yes, he flipped the switch.

You see, most religions are based on the works that we must do to try to be accepted by God. But Christianity is based, not on what I have done or must do, but on what God has already done in Christ. The sin problem is always based on our own free will. Mankind strives so hard to be the master of his own fate, but God did not make us that way. His plan is that we would choose, not our own way, but His way to live our lives. When Jesus came to this earth He made the statement, recorded for us in John 10:10, "I am come that you may have life, and have it more abundantly."

Jesus wants us to live an abundant life, resting in His grace and trusting in His mercy. Proverbs 3:5-6 says it so well: "Trust in the Lord with all your heart and lean not on your own understanding; in all your ways acknowledge Him, and He will make your paths straight." The opposite of trusting in the Lord is to lean on our own understanding. We like to figure things out for ourselves. We have an inner desire to solve our own problems, but there are those problems that come our way that are beyond our ability to solve. It's so much easier to do it God's way!

The question is, do I really trust Him? Or, can I really trust Him? To those who have trouble actually believing there is a God who loves them, I tell them, to pray every day for God to reveal Himself to you. If you pray that in all sincerity, He will reveal Himself to you! After all, He died for you, and He loves you more than you can comprehend. There is no reason for a seeking soul and a seeking Savior to be parted for long.

Now this plan of salvation God has challenged us with is quite simple and yet complicated at the same time. Jesus alludes to that in a parable He shares in Mark 4:26-29, "This is what the kingdom of God is like. A man scatters seed on the ground. Night and day, whether he sleeps or gets up, the seed sprouts and grows, though he does not know how. All by itself the soil produces grain – first the stalk, then the head, then the full kernel in the head. As soon as the grain is ripe, he puts the sickle to it, because the harvest has come."

There is so much about our relationship with Christ that we really don't or cannot understand, but we do experience the reality of it all. We accept it all as a part of our faith. Our lives are like that too. I don't understand how electricity works, but I still depend on it. I don't understand how we can put people on the moon, but God has created such a perfect world and man has found a way to calculate the mathematics of space travel so we are able to experience space travel.

This idea of trust, or faith, really begins with the cross. When I choose to believe that Jesus, as the Son of God, came to this earth for the express purpose of dying on an old rugged cross for my sin; that is the beginning of my faith journey. I love the old hymn "At The Cross" because the chorus explains what happens when I exercise faith in what Jesus did for me there. The chorus says, "At the cross, at the cross where I first saw the light, and the burden of my soul rolled away. It was there <u>by faith</u> I received my, sight, and now I am happy all the day."

So what happened to me when I embraced that cross? I saw the light of God's great plan, and the burden of sin that I carried "rolled away." That reminds me of a scene from the film "Pilgrim's Progress." Christian is ending his journey climbing a large mountain with the cross at the top. And as he climbs, there is a large bundle, or burden, on his back. Just as he nears the top, the burden on his back drops off and goes bounding down the hill. I get blessed every time I view that scene for that is just what happened to me. And then the chorus ends by saying, "It was there by faith I received my sight, and now I am happy all the day." Now I am able to see things clearly, and in so doing I experience happiness throughout the day.

The happiness that God gives us throughout the day really is an expression of the hope that is ours in Christ. Paul writes in Romans

15:13, "May the God of hope fill you with all joy and peace as you trust in Him, so that you may overflow with hope by the power of the Holy Spirit." Consider the wonderful words that Paul uses here: Hope, joy, peace, trust, overflow. You see, I must come to realize that Jesus really is who He claimed to be – the very Son of God.! As has been said in several ways, "Either Jesus is exactly who He said He was, or He is the greatest lunatic that ever lived." Jesus actually claimed to be the Son of God. Either that's who He is, or He is a liar!

One of the greatest pictures of trust found in the Bible is recorded for us in Luke 7:1-10. A Gentile, a military leader, had a servant who was very sick, actually facing death. This military leader, or centurion as he is called, had heard about Jesus and the miracles He was performing, but as a Gentile, he did not feel worthy to approach Jesus, so he sent some Jewish elders to ask Jesus to come and heal his servant. They went to Jesus and begged Him to come with them to the centurion's home. Jesus consented to go, but when they came near to the house, the centurion sent others to meet Jesus and say to Him, "I do not deserve for You to come under my roof, just say the word and my servant will be healed!" Jesus turned to the crowd who was following them and He said, "I have not found such great faith (trust) even in Israel!" And in that moment the servant was healed.

The centurion said, "Just say the word!" My trust and my faith always rest in the words of Jesus, then my daily actions must rest in the very words of Jesus! I may say I believe in Him, but do my actions validate what I say I believe?

QUESTIONS FOR DISCUSSION

1. Everyone trusts in something. What do you really trust?

2. There are certain things I say I believe, but do my actions show that what I say I believe is really true?

3. Am I relying on my own works, or, am I relying on what God has already done?

Chapter 4:
To Obey Or Not To Obey, That Is The Question?

It seems to me that if we really put our trust in God, then it would be natural to want to obey Him. But that doesn't seem to be the case. In the Old Testament, the Israelites had an awful time obeying the righteous standard God put before them. They would obey for a period of time and then slowly slide back into disobedience. And during that time they were under a sacrificial system whereby various animals were used as sacrifices for the sins of the people. But even then, when King Saul disobeyed the Lord, Samuel the prophet, said to him, "To obey is better than sacrifice." (I Samuel 15:22)

Now to walk in obedience to our God is really a joy. It is not a burdensome thing and there is a simplicity to it all. Our God is the best friend we have. There are three verses in II Thessalonians, chapter 5 that I call "The triangle of a victorious life in Christ."

Verses 16-18, "Be joyful always; pray continually; give thanks in all circumstances, for this is God's will for you in Christ Jesus." Three simple commands: Be joyful – be prayerful – be thankful!

"Be joyful." I love to be around joyful people. I love to worship God in a service that is full of joy. An older man was wearing a shirt that read: "I am not 80 years old; I am a sweet 16 with 74 years of experience." Joy is an attitude of the heart, and Jesus has promised to fill us with His joy.

"Pray continually." The Apostle Paul admonishes us to pray without ceasing. How do we do that? Again, I think it is an attitude of the heart. It is possible to live each day in constant communion with our heavenly Father. It is also a way to deal with temptation, and that is to turn every tempting thought into a conversation with God.

"Be thankful." The progression of sin that Paul writes about in the first chapter of Romans tells us that it all begins with an ungrateful spirit. Romans 1:21 says, "For although they knew God, they neither glorified Him as God nor gave thanks to Him, but their thinking became futile and their foolish hearts were darkened." They did not glorify God, and they were not thankful!

In Jeremiah 7:23-24 Jeremiah says to the people, "Obey Me and I will be your God and you will be My people. Walk in all the ways I command you, that it may go well with you." In Jeremiah 11:7, he says to them again, "From the time I brought your forefathers up from Egypt until today, I warned them again and again, saying, 'Obey Me.'" Obedience is crucial to a healthy relationship with the Lord!

And God's righteous standard was not given by God as some arbitrary list of rules to make people's lives miserable. These laws were given so that God's people might experience the very fullness of life. These commands were given for their benefit. In Deuteronomy 26:17-19 we have a description of God's reasoning – "You have declared this day that the Lord is your God and that you will walk in His ways, that you will keep His decrees, commands, and laws, and that you will obey Him. And the Lord has declared this day that you are His people, His treasured possession as He promised and that you are to keep all His commands. He has declared that He will set you in praise, fame, and honor high above all the nations He has made and that you will be a people holy to the Lord your God, as He promised."

When I read that, I said to myself, "Wow!" What an awesome relationship God desired to have with His people! If they would only love Him, and obey Him, He would make them to be delight in the plans He had outlined for them. Now this scripture says that the people had declared that they would serve and obey the Lord. That did happen, for a time. But then, the people began to get their priorities out of kilter. They began to relegate God to second place, or even lower in their lives.

Then came the time when God ordained Joshua to lead the Israelites across the Jordan River and into the Promised Land. Soon after, Joshua had to challenge them relative to their priorities. In Joshua 24:14-15 Joshua said to the people, "Now fear the Lord and serve Him with all faithfulness. Throw away the gods your forefathers worshiped beyond the River and in Egypt, and serve the Lord. But if serving the Lord seems undesirable to you, then choose for yourselves this day whom you will serve, whether the gods your forefathers served beyond the River or the gods of the Amorites, in whose land you are living. But as for me and my household, we will serve the Lord."

In essence, Joshua drew a line in the sand. He said, "Today, I want you to make up your minds exactly who you will serve. Quit vacillating. Make up your mind now! I've already made up mine. As for me and my house, we will serve the Lord!"

Now there are other things that mess up our priorities, other than who it is that we worship. There are those times when we think we know better than God the path we should take. In First Samuel, we have the story of Saul, who thought it was alright to do his own thing rather than to do what God said. On this occasion, Saul was supposed to wait for Samuel the prophet plus doing some other things God had commanded. But after all, he was king – he decided to do his own thing. But when Samuel got there and saw what Saul had done, Samuel said to him in I Samuel 15:22, "To obey is better than sacrifice."

Now it's impossible to obey if we are not in God's Word. The Bible gives us the instructions we need if we are going to be obedient children of God. I need to saturate my life with the Word of God. What if we treated our Bibles the way we treat our cell phones? We carry them with us wherever we go. We check them for messages throughout the day. We use them when we find ourselves in some emergency. And we often spend an hour or more in them every single day. To do this with the

Word of God would really make a difference in our lives.

The Word of God is the only thing we have that is totally inspired by God Himself. It doesn't tell us about the truth, it is the Truth. It doesn't just contain words about God; it is the Word of God. We don't have to try hard to make it relevant; it is relevant. Don't neglect it! We may neglect our home or our garden, but we dare not neglect God's Word. It is the foundation of our spiritual life. It feeds our faith. We live in a world that is not our home. We live as pilgrims on a journey in another land. And if we really want to know how to live as aliens in this strange country, the Bible is the answer!

When we consider the life of Jesus while He was on this earth, He is the perfect example of obedience to the Father. Jesus prayed to His Father often. He told His disciples that the things He did, and the words He said came directly from the Father. The author of Hebrews writes this in Hebrews 5:8-9, "Although He was a Son, He learned obedience from what He suffered and, once made perfect, He became the source of eternal salvation for all who obey Him." Jesus is our supreme example!

The relationships we share within our families are a picture of the relationships we share within the Family of God. What a delight it is to see children who act in obedience to the wishes of their parents. The Bible tells us that a rebellious son brings heartache to his mother. Likewise, a rebellious Christian is likely not a Christian at all!

We have all seen children who have been raised in a very permissive home without any discipline. They turn out to be very self-centered in their decision-making process. On the other hand, when children are raised in an environment where there is a combination of genuine love and discipline, their chance for success in life is greatly enhanced. True discipline prepares us in a greater measure for all of the things life throws at us.

When we talk about obedience, it is important to understand what Jesus said to His disciples after His resurrection. You see, His resurrection changed everything! Matthew's gospel, chapter 28, verses 16-20, shows us a stunning picture. "Then the eleven disciples went to Galilee, to the mountain where Jesus had told them to go. When they saw Him, they worshiped Him; but some doubted. Then Jesus came to them and said, 'All authority in heaven and on earth has been given to Me. Therefore go and make disciples of all nations, baptizing them in the name of the Father and of the Son and of the Holy Spirit, and teaching them to obey everything I have commanded you. And surely I am with you always, to the very end of the age.'"

When Jesus says, "All authority in heaven and on earth has been given to Me," there is no higher authority than that! That says to me, "I can trust Him – I am wise to trust Him, so when He asks me to do something, I should do it!" We call this The Great Commission. In it, Jesus is saying, "Go and make disciples, baptize them, and teach them all about Me."

You see, as we learn to trust Him, we also learn to obey Him and to represent Him to our world. As we surrender to Him, He gives us a mission – to share what we have experienced with others. The problem is, we come up with all kinds of excuses: I'm not smart enough. I'm too young. I'm too old. I'm not ready. My neighbors will make fun of me. I'm not trained. But when Jesus says, "All authority has been given to Me, now you go in My name," folks that's the biggest and greatest challenge you have ever been given. The greatest worship we will ever give Him is our obedience!

These two words that I have been writing about, trust and obedience, are at the heart of our relationship with God. They encompass all that really matters in this faith journey we are a part of. And when we think of Jesus's death on the cross, it wasn't the nails that held Him to the cross, it was His love for the Father, and His obedience to the Father, and His love for us! Our love for God should always be the foundation for our obedience. Our obedience should flow out of our love. In fact, it is our love for God that is really the basis for both our Trust and our Obedience!

And we need to remember that our love for God begins with the love He has for us. Like one of the old hymns says, "I love Him because He first loved me." And I love the verse of scripture that is found in I John 3:1, "How great is the love the Father has lavished on us, that we should be called children of God! And that is what we are!"

I love the word "lavished" as it is used in one of the more modern translations. Picture with me if you will a very large dump truck – about sixty feet tall and a hundred feet long. Watch as it pulls into heaven's portals, and God begins to fill it with His love. When He is done, His load of love is overflowing on all sides. Then watch as that huge truck comes to your house, and as you walk out the front door, it backs up to where you are and dumps that load of God's love all over you. If you can really picture that scene, then you should never doubt God's love ever again.

Now since the idea for this book came from that great hymn "Trust and Obey" I want to wrap things up with my own testimony. My own testimony is expressed in the fourth verse of that hymn. "But we never can prove the delights of His love until all on the altar we lay, for the favor He shows and the joy He bestows are for them who will trust and obey."

My testimony relative to trusting God and obeying Him began in my second year of college when the college I was attending experienced a real revival on the campus. This revival took place during a spiritual emphasis week with special chapel services every day of that week. It all culminated on Friday morning, when, during the worship time of the chapel service, students began to move to the altar. As I watched all of this happen I felt an urge to go forward myself. But I hesitated at first. I couldn't think of anything specific that I needed to pray about, but the urge to go forward became stronger. So I yielded. I moved to the altar.

Now there were so many students gathered in prayer at the front of the auditorium that none of my friends saw me there at the altar praying. But it was while I knelt there in God's presence that I felt a call to full-time ministry. I can't explain it, but it is as real today as it was back then. I have never doubted my call to ministry. The problem was, that I really did not have the gifts for ministry. I was an introvert with a very poor self-image. I was unable to speak in front of people, so a call to ministry made no sense to me. So I said to the Lord, "Lord Jesus, I am definitely experiencing a call to the pastoral ministry, but my personality does not fit that kind of a call. So my response is this: I promise to follow your direction wherever you lead; as You open the doors, I will walk through them, but I am not pushing any doors open. You will have to make Your will very clear."

It was one week later; all of my unit mates were in bed asleep, so in the quietness of the moment I decided to take a shower. As I was showering, someone knocked on my shower door. I opened the door to see one of the dorm supervisors standing there. He said, "I'm sorry to bother you so late and in the shower, but I need someone to go down to Hollywood High School in the morning and speak to some students that meet every Friday morning in a little church across the street from the High School." I responded, "Why me? I'm not a ministerial student!" He said, "I don't know why you, I just couldn't get you out of my mind." About that time God said, "You said, 'If I open the doors you would walk through them.'" I said yes I would do it, and God really helped me that next morning.

My life since that Friday morning has been unbelievable! God began opening doors from that very moment. I have done so many things I never would have thought possible. Like another old hymn says, "Jesus Led Me All The Way." And the key to all of it was in those two words, Trust and Obey! So simple, yet so profound!

QUESTIONS FOR DISCUSSION

1. Our obedience is always tied to God's directives in the Scriptures. God never leads contrary to Scripture. God always means what He says! Is it hard for you to obey someone other than yourself?

2. Think about this: I obey God's directives because I know the depth of His love! Consider this scripture in I John 3:1, "See what great love the Father has lavished on us, that we should be called children of God! And that is what we are!" Just try to define the word "lavished."

Chapter 5:
God Is Pro-Choice

When we talk about "trust" and "obedience" there is a real connection in those two words to the freedoms we have in our relationship with God. The Apostle Paul had a lot to say about our freedom in Christ. He wrote in Romans 8:1-2, "Therefore, there is now no condemnation for those who are in Christ Jesus because through Christ Jesus the law of the Spirit who gives life has set you free from the law of sin and death."

Now we must understand that genuine freedom is not a freedom to do anything we want to do! True freedom means that we are free to become the best we can become. We do those things that enhance our success in life, especially in the relationships we share with others.

When God created man, the greatest thing He gave him was the freedom to choose. And in the very beginning, God placed man in a beautiful garden with all kinds of fruit-bearing trees. But there was one tree in the middle of the garden that God told man not to touch at all. But the choice was still there! God did not want the man He created to be a puppet who would always do His bidding. No, He wanted man to choose to trust, and obey what God wanted for him.

We live in a day and age where our society is so divided when it comes to the issue of abortion. Some are pro-choice and others are pro-life. But when we look at these two positions from a biblical perspective, we need to realize that a biblical worldview means we are both pro-choice and pro-life.

God is truly the author of the pro-choice movement, and He is also very pro-life. God has given us the freedom to make our own choices. We are the only thing God created that has the freedom to reject God's divine plan for us. We can say to God, "I don't want to abide by Your precepts and rules. I want to do my own thing." And God respects our decisions.

You see, when God gave the Ten Commandments, they weren't given to make our lives miserable, they were given to guide and direct our lives so we could be the best possible persons we could be. Our lives truly become a result of the many choices we have made throughout our lives.

When we go to a doctor we want him to tell us what things we need to do to live healthy lives. And so, he gives us directions that usually involve exercise, diet, and often medication of some kind.

Now we have a choice. Do we take seriously what the doctor has told us? Do we begin to exercise more? Do we change our diet? Do we take our medications? How many of you have purchased a treadmill that now sits in your garage, or you sold in a garage sale? How many of us have started diets that lasted less than a month? Do you eat what you want to eat, or do you eat what you ought to eat?

Well God in His great wisdom has laid out directives for us to follow that will result in the best possible life I could ever live. In the Old Testament Joshua, as a leader in Israel, called all of the people together and said to them, "Choose you this day whom you will serve. If God is really God, then choose Him, but if you prefer the false gods you now serve, then serve them, but as for me and my house we will serve the Lord." (Joshua 24:14-15)

Yes, God is the author of the pro-choice movement. But He is also the author of the pro-life movement. Jesus said in John 19:10, "I am come that you may have life, and have it more abundantly." That means that God's plan for us is a full and meaningful life!

All through life we are called upon to make choices. Some of the most important are: What will I do with my life? What vocation will I choose? And who will I marry? When marriage is proposed, the question is, is this the person I want to partner with for life, or is this the partner God wants me to share my life with? God does lead and give direction for all of those major choices we must make.

So when I hear people say, "I have the freedom to do whatever I want to do with my own body?" That's only partly true. God is the giver of life, and He always chooses life not death. So true freedom is showing respect for what God has told me is right. The true choice is made before conception happens.

As I make my way through this life, my goal is to always make decisions based on a biblical worldview. In other words, I want what God wants for me. I want to echo the position Joshua took – "As for me, and my house, we will serve the Lord!"

~⸎

Chapter 6:
Postscript

I have lived my life doing my best to exemplify a child-like faith in all of the decisions I make. A couple of years ago I decided to write a letter to all of my grandchildren encouraging them to follow my example. And since we are God's children, we are all part of His great big, wonderful family. So this letter I wrote to my grandchildren, is also for you! Here is that letter.....

"Today, Good Friday, we celebrate the day Jesus went to the cross. That event is the basis for everything I believe in. Knowing that I am nearing the finish line of my life's race, I decided to write an open letter to all of my grandchildren. You all are very loved by your grandmother and me. Also, we have two of my grandchildren who are soon to graduate from High School and have made plans to go on to college. Knowing that what happens in college often challenges many of the beliefs we have grown up with, I want all of my grandchildren to understand just how wonderful it is to make Jesus Christ the Lord of your life. I have lived my whole life in a special relationship with my Lord and Savior, and I don't regret one day of it. He has truly been wonderful to me!

There is nothing that will enable you to meet life's many problems more than living life with a Biblical worldview! The Bible is the source for all of the answers we need to live our lives successfully. Mankind has tried to destroy the Bible ever since it was written and yet it has still been the best-selling book for hundreds of years.

There are four reasons that make up the foundation for my faith. First of all, the Creation of this world of ours. This world functions with such precision and beauty. There is no way I could come to the conclusion that all of this came to be by accident. There is definitely a Master Designer, and we owe our very existence to Him.

The second reason is the Jewish nation. Of all the people on this planet, God chose a people through whom He would make Himself known to His world. And when this nation strayed away from God's divine plan, God scattered them to the ends of the earth for over 400 years without anywhere to call home. But God's prophecy was that one day they would come back together and once again be a formable nation. That happened in 1948 to everyone's amazement.

My third reason is the Bible itself. It has proven itself true over and over again. I have experienced the fulfillment of its promises over and over again in my life. This leads to the fourth reason, which is my personal experience with the Lord Jesus Christ. God has met the needs of our family over and over again. I have written three books about it. It has truly been an awesome journey, and I would recommend it to anyone searching for the Truth.

So, when the time comes for me to leave this world, I want you to know exactly where I am going. There is an eternal home prepared for me over in glory, where I will see Jesus face to face. And my utmost desire is that I would meet every one of you there someday. Don't allow yourself to be sidetracked by the false belief system of this world. Satan is also real, and he will try everything under the sun to side-track your own faith. Stay true to Him who loved you so much that He gave His life for you on this weekend some 2,000 years ago."

I love you all very much,

Grandpa Eckdahl